Test Your Dog

HarperCollins*Publishers*
I London Bridge Street
London SEI 9GF

www.harpercollins.co.uk

HarperCollinsPublishers
Ist Floor, Watemarque Building, Ringsend Road
Dublin 4, Ireland

First published by Barnes and Noble by
arrangement with HarperCollins*Publishers*
This edition published by HarperCollins*Publishers* 2017

19

© Harper Collins 2008
Text by Rachel Federman
Illustrations by Gary Bennett
Interior design by Rosamund Saunders
Cover images © Shutterstock

A catalogue record for this book is available from the British Library

ISBN 978-0-00-814965-9

Printed and Bound in the UK using 100% Renewable Electricity at
CPI Group (UK) Ltd

MIX
Paper from
responsible sources
FSC
www.fsc.org
FSC™ C007454

This book is produced from independently certified FSC™ paper
to ensure responsible forest management.

For more information visit: www.harpercollins.co.uk/green

Test Your Dog

THE DOG IQ TEST

Is Your Dog an Undiscovered Genius?

RACHEL FEDERMAN

ILLUSTRATIONS BY GARY BENNETT

HarperCollins*Publishers*

Foreword

A rough diamond is better than a perfect pebble.

Everyone has beauty but not everyone sees it.

Chinese proverbs contain the essence of philosophy in so few yet such wise words, which always captivate me. It's like life lessons in an instant. These are two of my favourites, and for me, they sum up the question of canine intelligence. Every dog is unequivocally, unashamedly itself, and has its own unique IQ, and. The question is, are we as simple humans smart enough to recognise it?

When a little stray dog followed me as I ran a 155-mile race across the Gobi Desert in the vast, arid region of Northern China, I could have questioned her intelligence.

The Gobi Desert is know for its sand dunes, mountains and lack of human habitation, so what on earth was this tiny dog thinking running in the heat of the desert alongside me, in the most extreme conditions, without any water or food, but also without a care in the world? Of course I could have asked myself the same questions.

It turns out that Gobi, as I would later name her, was pretty smart indeed – she chose the right person to follow and now lives a completely different life nearly 5000 miles away at my home in Edinburgh, Scotland. Why did Gobi choose me? What was she doing in the desert? What was she surviving on? Only Gobi knows the answers to these questions, but her survival is a testament to her incredible intelligence, good judgment, adaptability, resilience and inbuilt canine survival skills.

Gobi's unbelievable achievement of running 77 miles in the race across the desert is undoubtedly her biggest trick. Gobi doesn't know how to sit, roll over or fetch, but she can most definitely run! Intelligence, just like in any human, is different in every dog. Learning your dog's capabilities and limitations is not only a fun exercise to complete, but can enhance your relationship with your pooch.

Whether your pup is the next Einstein or not isn't really the point. After all, humans play a big role in developing a dog's IQ, and we aren't always the smartest… Our canine companions are every bit as intelligent as we know them to be in our hearts, and just as intelligent as they need to be.

Dion Leonard
Author of *Finding Gobi*

"I used to look at [my dog] Smokey and think, 'If you were a little smarter you could tell me what you were thinking,' and he'd look at me like he was saying, 'If you were a little smarter, I wouldn't have to.'"

Fred Jungclaus

Contents

Acknowledgments

Thanks to Jeannine Dillon and Erica Heisman, my lovely editors; Gary Bennett for bringing the text to life with his charming illustrations; all the dog owners who graciously gave their time to take the test in the beta stage; and Bear, Bella, Biskit, Bronx, Brutus, Casey, Chloe, Cody Nick, Crumpet, Echo, Jenny, Jonas, Lady, Mac, Maddy, Max, Mimi, Nay Nay, Olive, Pal, Patti Smith, Petit, Porter, Raster, Remi, Rugby, Sequoyah, Skye, Spencer, Teca, Tippy, Tyler, and Uncle Sam, and all the other wonderful sheep in wolves' clothing who make or made every day better, asking so little in return.

In loving memory of Casey who would have surely aced the dog IQ test.

Introduction

By the time babies are one year old, the act of sitting is unlikely to be met with much fanfare. As guests we're told to *have a seat,* in church to *be seated,* as stragglers at the movies to get *down in front.* Otherwise, we'd be reluctant to sit on command, even if someone was waving a giant piece of cheesecake in the air.

Dogs can sit much earlier than we can, yet a dog that will sit on command – outside and in the company of other energetic dogs – is a wonder to be marvelled at. A well-trained dog is seen as a smart dog, and therein lies the essential difficulty of determining a dog's IQ.

And because the only use dogs have for a pencil is as a barely adequate chew toy, it's hard for us to get a clear picture of what goes on inside their furry heads.

It's especially tricky to compare one dog to another because the differences between breeds are great. The difference between a mastiff and a Chihuahua, for example, may be greater than the difference between your dim-witted brother-in-law and Koko, the "talking" gorilla. Think of the surprise and disappointment of a family who hoped a golden retriever would serve as a watchdog, or the disaster of thinking a Bijon Frise would help on a hunt.

Dogs, though they share many traits with their wild ancestors, have been bred by humans to act in particular ways and many now barely resemble each other, in personality or appearance.

So a single test can't fully assess the variance across different breeds, while taking into account early life and training. An obedient dog brought up in the Police Academy is not necessarily inherently smarter than a wild dog who grew up on a council estate.

The question this test addresses then is not "Does my dog have the capacity to understand complex numbers?" but rather "Can my dog function effectively in our world?" Aeons ago, a lazy couch potato dog – perfect for life in an apartment today – would have been the weakest member of the pack, just as today's brilliant physicist might have been a huge liability for hunter-gatherers in the Stone Age. For any species, an intelligence test is context dependent. Today's standardized intelligence tests for humans are attacked for ignoring that fact.

Intelligence in dogs can be categorized into four basic areas: communication skills, social behavior, perceptual/motor skills, and memory and association. The higher order functions of judgment and resilience also factor into our understanding of canine aptitude.

In designing this test, I've relied on Robert J. Sternberg's *Triarchic Theory of (Human) Intelligence* which has been broadly applied to studies of canine IQ. Following Sternberg, I define intelligence as one's ability to achieve a desired goal in one's environment. After all, a border collie that's a genius on a Scottish farm has a thing or two to learn before he will impress the poodles in the cafes along the Champs-Elysées.

This test is not a rigorous intelligence standard compiled by a group of scientists huddled around their panting subjects and a massive pile of treats. It's merely a fun gauge for adoring dog owners to see how adaptable, understanding, and yes, intelligent their best friends really are.

Like a modern day Lassie, will your dog dial 999 if you fall and can't get up? Will he bark until help arrives? Will he lie down next to you? Or will he circle around his leash, hoping for a walk?

Fortunately, dogs make our task a bit easier than pets of the feline variety because they're so eager to please us. Once they understand what we're asking, they'll jump through hoops for an "atta boy," which, when you stop to think about it, isn't that much different than humans, depending on who is handing out the praise.

Most importantly, your dog needs a patient owner willing to take the time to show him the ropes of domestic life. Otherwise you'll likely have a shredded sofa, peevish neighbours, and trouble getting valid results on this test.

THE
DOG
IQ
TEST

Day to Day with Your Dog
Part 1 – The Frequency Exam

Instructions

This first part of the test is based on observations you can make without consulting your dog. There are 15 questions in this section. Decide which level of frequency best describes your pet's behaviour by using the following scale:

> Always
> Sometimes
> Never

When you've finished this exam, refer to page 103 for the Rating Scale and mark each page with the number of points your dog earned for that question.

Does your dog recognize the signs that indicate you are preparing his or her food?

Always: ☐

Sometimes: ☐

Never: ☐

Points Received

_____

2

Does your dog have different reactions to different foods (e.g. is especially eager for a piece of salami vs. the same old dry food)?

Always: ☐

Sometimes: ☐

Never: ☐

Points Received

_____

3

Does your dog seek out water on hot days or after exercise?

Always: ☐

Sometimes: ☐

Never: ☐

Points Received

_____

23

4

If the place your dog typically takes a nap is unavailable, will he easily find an alternate spot?

Always: ☐

Sometimes: ☐

Never: ☐

Points Received

_____

5

Does your dog seem to understand signals that you're preparing for sleep and act accordingly?

Always: ☐

Sometimes: ☐

Never: ☐

Points Received

_____

6

If something unusual happens in the middle of the night (e.g. a loud crash or smoke alarm), does your dog attempt to rouse you by barking or putting a paw on your arm?

Always: ☐

Sometimes: ☐

Never: ☐

Points Received

_____

7

When your dog is uncomfortable, does he modify his environment (e.g. duck under a blanket if he is cold)?

Always: ☐

Sometimes: ☐

Never: ☐

Points Received

_____

31

8

When it's raining, is your dog less enthusiastic to go for a walk?

Always: ☐

Sometimes: ☐

Never: ☐

Points Received

_____

9

Does your dog's behaviour change during a thunderstorm?

Always: ☐

Sometimes: ☐

Never: ☐

Points Received

_____

10

When out on a walk and heading back to your house, does your dog automatically turn in at your driveway?

Always: ☐

Sometimes: ☐

Never: ☐

Points Received

_____

| |

Is your dog interested in new toys and challenges?

Always: ☐

Sometimes: ☐

Never: ☐

Points Received

_____

12

If your dog does something wrong and is reprimanded, does he show signs of remorse (e.g. tail between legs, averting eye contact)?

Always: ☐

Sometimes: ☐

Never: ☐

Points Received

_____

13

If your dog does something wrong but has *not* yet been reprimanded, does he show signs of remorse?

Always: ☐

Sometimes: ☐

Never: ☐

Points Received

_____

14

Does your dog recognize friends upon first sight/smell?

Always: ☐

Sometimes: ☐

Never: ☐

Points Received

_____

15

Does your dog inspect new objects
(e.g. a box that arrives in the mail or a new
piece of furniture)?

Always: ☐

Sometimes: ☐

Never: ☐

Points Received

_____

Canine Capabilities
Part 2 – The Situational Exam

Instructions

The Situational Exam is a standard multiple choice test consisting of 15 questions. Select the answer that most closely matches your dog's actions or personality. When you've finished this exam, refer to page 103 for the Rating Scale and mark each page with the number of points your dog earned for that question.

|

Training sessions with your dog are:

a. A picturesque scene of suburban ☐
   tranquillity

b. Hard to take, but ultimately rewarding ☐

c. The reason dog houses were invented ☐

Points Received

_____

2

What is your dog's level of word recognition?

a. He beats me at Scrabble ☐

b. He can make polite conversation ☐

c. I'm *pretty* sure he knows his name ☐

Points Received

_____

53

3

When you are packing to go on a trip, at what point does your dog show first signs of anxiety that you are leaving?

a. When I google "St. Tropez" ☐

b. As I am packing the bathing suit I'll never get the courage to wear ☐

c. I barely get a wave goodbye ☐

Points Received

4

Roughly how many tricks does your dog know?

a. David Blaine could learn a thing or two ☐

b. Enough to entertain party guests ☐

c. If I say "Sit" and push his butt down, ☐
   nine times out of ten he'll grudgingly
   oblige

Points Received

_____

5

When you call your dog's name in a happy, sing-song way does he:

a. Come running over ☐

b. Wag his tail or raise his ears ☐

c. Give you a look that's the canine equivalent of "*You talkin' to me?*" ☐

Points Received

_____

6

If your dog needs to relieve himself, how does he get your attention?

a. He'll wait patiently and hope you realize ☐ he's had to go since the *Star Trek* marathon started six hours ago

b. He'll approach you with his leash in his ☐ mouth or bark

c. He'll find your brand new carpet ☐ and make sure you don't make him wait again

Points Received

_____

61

7

When taking a walk does your dog show interest in new sights and sounds?

a. He mostly bobs along but checks out ☐
   a rubbish bin or neighbour's cat every
   block or so

b. If a group of Hells Angels rode by in a ☐
   Cinco De Mayo parade, he might look up

c. Yes, he is very active and aware ☐

Points Received

_____

63

8

If your dog were to end up on TV, would it most likely be:

a. As an easy task on *It's Me or the Dog* ☐

b. As Best-in-Breed at Crufts ☐

c. On National Geographic's *Wild Kingdom* ☐

Points Received

_____

9

If your dog is lying down – but not asleep –
and you clap your hands, does he:

a. Lift his head or make some
   acknowledgement that you exist ☐

b. Come over to where you are ☐

c. Continue staring dully into space ☐

Points Received

_____

10

If your dog wants to play, but you are busy does he:

a. Keep pestering you ☐

b. Play by himself ☐

c. Give up and watch *Blue's Clues* ☐

Points Received

_____

11

When your dog first enters a new space, does he:

a. Sniff around and explore or focus intently on a new object of interest ☐

b. Cling nervously to your side like an awkward adolescent ☐

c. Yap and growl at an unfamiliar object ☐

Points Received

_____

12

When you teach your dog a new trick does he:

a. Remember it as long as the liver treats last ☐

b. Perform it with aplomb for guests the next afternoon ☐

c. Pretend to have no idea what you're talking about, then do his best feline impersonation by making a regal exit down the hall ☐

Points Received

_____

13

When a friend your dog likes, but sees rarely, comes to visit, what is his reaction?

a. Shows extreme happiness when your ☐
   friend arrives

b. Shows hesitation at first but soon ☐
   shows signs of recognition

c. Acts as if your friend is on the FBI's ☐
   Most Wanted List

Points Received

_____

74

14

When you're not feeling well, your dog:

a. Lies quietly by your side ☐

b. Tries to cheer you up by pummelling ☐
   you with his slobbery toys

c. Shows the understanding of a traffic ☐
   warden as you feebly explain that you
   just ran into the store for a second

Points Received

_____

15

If your dog comes across another dog on a walk, what will he do?

a. Wave his tail, eager for a friendly meet and greet ☐

b. Lunge toward the dog, straining on the leash ☐
☐

c. Bark or growl ☐

Points Received

_____

Pooch Performance

Part 3 – The Activity Exam

Instructions

For the final part of the test you'll need your dog's participation. Choose a time when he's well rested and not distracted. The tasks can be spread out over several days to prevent mental or physical fatigue which could potentially affect the results. It's best not to conduct any drills or warm-ups before you begin.

When you've completed all 8 activity tests, refer to page 105 for the Rating Scale and mark each page with the number of points your dog earned for that question.

Materials

Stopwatch

Plastic cup

4–5 toys (can include homemade toys but you'll need one brand new one that you know will intrigue your dog)

Treat – small pieces of something your dog really loves and doesn't get every day such as cheese, peanut butter, or turkey. Peanut butter requires a willingness to get a little dirty on your part and a considerate dog who will lick rather than bite it off your finger. Most dogs know to do this – but just be aware if they get excited and keyed up around some of the tasks below. You'll also need one *wildly tempting treat* such as a piece of chicken or steak. Be sure to remove the bone.

83

Goal: To test innovation and dexterity.

Get your stopwatch ready. Show your dog that you have a treat in your hand (a small piece of cheese for example.) Next, put it under a plastic cup on the floor, and encourage your dog to go after it. How long does it take your dog to reach it?

a. Under 10 seconds ☐

b. 11 seconds – 2.59 minutes ☐

c. 3 – 10 minutes ☐

d. Tries, but can't figure it out ☐

e. What cup? ☐

Points Received

_____

85

2

Goal: To test understanding of hand gestures and your dog's sense of smell.

Select another treat and show your dog you have it in your hand. Next, close yourself in a room without your dog and "hide" it somewhere (place it somewhere rather obvious and within your dog's line of sight.) Next, let your dog in the room, show your empty hands and point to indicate he should look around. Your dog:

a. Runs directly to you assuming you have it even though you showed you do not ☐

b. Understands when you point that he should look around and finds it ☐

c. Understands when you point that he should look around but doesn't find it ☐

d. Follows his nose immediately to the treat ☐

e. Didn't follow you back into the room ☐

Points Received

———————————

3

Goal: To test short-term memory.

This time take the treat and show the dog where you are placing it in the room, but don't let him have it. Lead him out of the room, close the door and distract him with a few commands (sit / paw etc.) Now, open the door to the room and let your dog in. What does he do?

a. Runs directly to you assuming you have it even though you showed you do not ☐

b. Sniffs around and quickly finds the treat ☐

c. Sniffs around the room for several minutes or more until he finds the treat ☐

d. Searches without any luck ☐

e. He's still scratching his head over "sit" and "paw" ☐

Points Received

_____

4

Goal: To test understanding of delayed gratification.

Tell your dog to sit and stay about 10 feet from his food bowl. Next, put a handful of treats into the bowl, reminding your dog to stay. Get out your stopwatch and wait a full minute. If your dog has waited patiently, after one minute tell him "good dog" and let him get up to get the treat. Do not give any command to the dog until then, even if he disobeys in a most flagrant manner. What did he do?

a. Wait like an angel until you said he could get up ☐

b. Wait in a squirmy way, like a kid who spotted a tray of cupcakes before it's time for dessert ☐

c. Inch forward, staying low to the ground until he reached the bowl ☐

d. Stay in place for a good 10 seconds then run over to gobble the treat ☐

e. The treats didn't touch the bottom of the bowl ☐

Points Received

_____

5

Goal: To test obedience without supervision.

For this test you'll need the steak or other *wildly tempting treat* mentioned above. Leave it out on your kitchen counter (make sure the counter is otherwise clear) and exit the room (staying within earshot). Don't look at your dog with a cautionary face, and don't give him any commands. Leave the room for a good ten minutes if all is quiet. If you hear any noise, come back sooner. Where's the steak?

a. On the counter exactly as you left it ☐

b. On the counter surrounded by dirty paw mark ☐

c. On the floor where your dog dropped it like a hot ☐
   potato when you came back into the room

d. On the floor in the iron grip of your dog's pointy ☐
   choppers

e. On your lovely floral sofa, where your dog is ☐
   stretched out like a Roman Emperor having his cake
   and eating it too

Points Received

_____

6

Goal: To test response time to new information.

For this test your dog needs to be comfortably sleeping for at least a half hour. From another room, call your dog's name with a sense of urgency and clap your hands. What does he do?

a. Comes running within seconds ☐

b. Comes over after several calls and hand claps ☐

c. Cannot be coaxed out of bed until you go to the room and give him a few "wake up" pats on the back ☐

d. Cannot be coaxed up even when you give him a pat ☐

e. Gives you a look of disgust when you go into the room and wake him up, and promptly finds another spot to lie down, preferably out of your reach ☐

Points Received

_____

zzzzzzz

95

7

Goal: To test interest in new activities.

This test requires the purchase of a new toy. Keep the toy in the bag, and when you get home, make a big deal of how you have something fun in the bag for the dog. When you hold it out, your dog:

a. Grabs it and runs off to explore it alone ☐

b. Grabs it and tries to play together with you ☐

c. Touches it with his paw or sniffs it, showing mild interest ☐

d. Is too excited that you're home to notice a silly toy ☐

e. Lets out a long sigh that sounds vaguely like "You again?" followed by a lengthy gaze out the window ☐

Points Received

_____

8

Goal: To see if old dogs can learn new tricks.

Choose an area in the room that is *not* one of your dog's favorite spots. Designate the area with a name – it can be a made up word or a real name, but it should just be one word. We will use "table" for example, rather than "under the table" even though the physical area we mean is under the table. Using a treat, lure the dog over to the area and repeat the word when he gets there and as he eats the treat. Repeat this step three times in total. Now bring your dog at least 10 feet from the area and ask him to sit. Looking your dog in the eye and holding the treat, say "table" and wait. If there is no reaction, repeat the command and look in the direction of the table. Your dog:

a. Runs over to the area on the first command ☐

b. After several repetitions, he goes to the area ☐

c. Tries to grab the treat from your hand ☐

d. Whimpers and does a familiar trick (e.g. "paw") ☐

e. Would rather watch the clock tick ☐

Points Received

_____

Bonus!

Extra Credit Points

☐ Is your dog friendly with other friendly dogs? +2

☐ Do you feel comfortable letting your dog interact with
a lively child? +5

☐ Does your dog respond to hand gestures? +2

☐ Does your dog respond to facial signals? +3

☐ Is your dog equally obedient and able to perform tricks
both outside and inside? +8

Bonus Points Received

_____

Rating Scale –
Scoring the Dog IQ Test

THE FREQUENCY EXAM – POINTS EARNED
Questions 1–15

a) 4 points

b) 2 points

c) 0 points

Total Number of Points for the Frequency Exam:

_____ points

THE SITUATIONAL EXAM – POINTS EARNED
Questions 1–5

a) 4 points

b) 3 points

c) 2 points

Question 6

a) 4 points

b) 4 points

c) 2 points

Question 7

a) 3 points

b) 2 points

c) 4 points

Question 8

a) 3 points

b) 4 points

c) 2 points

Question 9

a) 3 points

b) 4 points

c) 2 points

Question 10

a) 2 points

b) 4 points

c) 3 points

Question 11

a) 4 points

b) 3 points

c) 2 points

Question 12

a) 3 points

b) 4 points

c) 2 points

Questions 13–15

a) 4 points

b) 3 points

c) 2 points

Total Number of Points for the Situational Exam:

_____ points

THE ACTIVITY EXAM – POINTS EARNED

Activity Test 1
- a) 4 points
- b) 3 points
- c) 2 points
- d) 1 point
- e) 0 points

Activity Test 2
- a) 1 point
- b) 4 points
- c) 2 points
- d) 4 points
- e) 0 points

Activity Tests 3
- a) 4 points
- b) 3 points
- c) 2 points
- d) 1 point
- e) 0 points

Activity Test 4
- a) 4 points
- b) 3 points
- c) 1 point
- d) 2 points
- e) 0 points

Activity Tests 5 and 6
- a) 4 points
- b) 3 points
- c) 2 points
- d) 1 point
- e) 0 points

Activity Test 7	**Activity Test 8**
a) 3 points	a) 4 points
b) 4 points	b) 3 points
c) 2 points	c) 1 point
d) 1 point	d) 2 points
e) 0 points	e) 0 points

Total Number of Points for the Activity Exam:

_____ points

Add together the number of points your dog earned in each of the exams and mark the subtotals below. Be sure and add in any extra credit your dog might have received in the bonus section. Add the four scores together and this will give you your dog's total IQ score.

Frequency Exam   _____

Situational Exam   _____

Activity Exam   _____

Extra Credit Points   _____

Total   _____

Take the **total number** you calculated above, and turn the page
to see where your dog lies in the range of canine intelligence.

Dog IQ Categories

Total Test Score	Category
155+	Genius
130–154	Superior
110–129	Above Average
90–109	Average
71–89	Slightly Below Average
70 or Below	Below Average

Analysing Your Dog's Score

You now have something to substantiate your late-night bravado about how much smarter your dog is than the mangy mutt next door. Or maybe you came up with a score that will send you scurrying to the Yellow Pages for dog trainers in the area. Either way, when reviewing what your dog's score means, keep in mind that many variables will influence the outcome, including age, health, exercise, and socialization. Though it's true you can't turn a pooch with the brainpower of a sweet potato into a prize-winner, the most important variable affecting your dog's score is the way he was raised and the environment he was raised in. In other words, *you* play a huge part in determining the final score. The text on the next page describes each category of intelligence, and the section that follows provides tips for improving your dog's score.

Genius (155+ Points)

Congratulations! If your dog were a human he might have Michel-angelo's artistic vision, Freud's insight into human behaviour, or Hemingway's gift for telling a story. Your dog is a model canine, the envy of your neighbours, the centre of attention in the park. He effortlessly learns new tricks, adjusts to new situations, helps you out of scrapes, and will one day accomplish great things.

Superior (130–154 Points)

Your dog is a highly intelligent and adaptable creature. He can easily form bonds with other dogs and humans, has no behavi-oural difficulties, responds quickly and appropriately to both new and familiar situations, enjoys puzzles and games and is a star companion.

Above Average (110–129 Points)

Your dog is bright, well socialized and well trained, able to assess most situations accurately, and incorporates and learns new skills without strain. He maintains good relationships with dogs and humans and will respond well to additional training.

Average (90–109 Points)

Your dog is likely to be an amiable and easy-going pet, able to be reigned in *most* of the time. With effort on your part he is house trained and able to conduct himself with good manners and function happily in his routine.

Slightly Below Average (71–89 Points)

Your pet needs extra time and attention to get to where he'll be happiest and cause the least trouble. If he's still young, he may show significant improvement as he ages and his puppy-like energy and lack of restraint begin to give way to a calmer demeanour.

Below Average (70 or Below Points)

If your pet were a student, he would need extra help in school, study group, *and* after-school activities. It's imperative that you give him the canine equivalent so he won't become difficult and can function happily and well on a day-to-day basis. All of which leads us to the following section.

How To Improve
Your Dog's Performance

For any dog to score well on an intelligence test, he needs proper training and care. You can improve his intelligence score by leading him through exercises like the ones in the Activity Exam or others you can find in basic training guides. A personal dog trainer is a great idea as well; it's true they train the humans, but we're the ones who need the training.

When teaching basic commands like *sit, paw, lie down, stay,* and *come here,* it's important to reward the dog instantly upon correct performance. A few seconds too late and you've missed the boat. Don't reward the dog when he fakes it, lazily half-sitting in hope of a treat. If you're using actual treats, give one every three correct tricks or so. Many dogs will be just as happy with a pat on the head and a "good dog." Start training inside and move outside when your dog is ready, using an extra long leash for teaching "stay" and adding distractions such as standing close to other dogs and shaking the leash as your dog sits patiently until you say "good dog" to signal completion of the task.

Most importantly, you'll need to look at the scope of your dog's existence and make sure his needs are being met, his boundaries are clear, and the environment is one he can thrive in. In the meantime, here are some tips for helping your furry friend reach his full potential:

Exercise

Your dog needs plenty of exercise – a minimum two half-hour walks daily, in addition to trips outside to relieve himself, taking into consideration age and health. You'll be amazed at the drastic change in your pooch's temperament when he gets the chance to burn that excess energy outside and not in a way that involves your white Italian leather sofa. If you don't have an off-leash park nearby where he can run loose, try to jog or do short sprints with him on the leash. Many experts feel that adequate exercise (which very few dogs get) will solve at least **90%** of behavioural problems.

Nutrition

Get the most nutritious dog food you can find. It doesn't have to be fancy, just healthy. Don't confuse your dog by slipping him pieces of your dinner under the table, but if you can give him human-grade food, so much the better. "You are what you eat" applies to canines as well as humans, and many readily available dog foods are packed with unhealthy by-products, corn syrup, and other junk we would never serve our in-laws let alone our best friends. It's also very important to provide fresh water throughout the day.

Schedule

All living creatures are happiest when living in sync with the Circadian Rhythm. Feed and walk your dog at the same time every day. If you go to bed and get up at roughly the same time, chances are your dog will too, and you'll both be better off. As many a self-help book will tell you, lack of sleep is less often the problem than an erratic schedule.

Stimulation

Provide your dog with plenty of toys and new stimulation. They don't have to be the store-bought variety. Be creative. You probably have items lying around that he'd love to get his claws on: old towels he's allowed to chew up (make sure he knows the difference between these and the monogrammed set from Harrods), sticks for him to chase, balls for him to swat around. Make sure whatever you give him is safe, without parts that could catch in his throat. And if you can afford it, pet stores have a wonderful array of puzzle toys to keep your dog occupied and inspired.

It's also important that you and other family members take time to play with your dog. Whether it's tug of war, fetch, Frisbee, swimming together, hide and seek – dogs are playful and social creatures and need to engage with others to operate at their full mental and physical capacity. Keep introducing your dog to new people, new dogs, new places, and new experiences and you'll keep his mind active and senses sharp.

Boundaries

In all these areas, you have to make the boundaries clear for your dog. He has to know where he's supposed to eat, where he's allowed to take a nap, how he's supposed to act around guests, etc. You can't let him jump up and "hug" you when you come home, but yell at him when he does the same to visitors. You can't let him climb up on the dining room table "just this once" because it's such a cute image but grow enraged when he does it on Thanksgiving. These distinctions we make all the time are completely arbitrary and will end up confusing your dog.

Make sure you are calm and in control at all times. Don't think that by indulging your wily sidekick you are doing him any favours. If he steals your spot, gently but assertively make him get out of it. If he takes your sweater and tries to play with it, make him let go and find a more appropriate toy. Remember how much you respected and trusted teachers who didn't let you get away with your miscreant ways? By setting fair rules and keeping to them, you'll show your dog you're a strong leader who will take care of him so that he can relax and live a dog's life.

The Canine Existentialist

No matter what your dog's IQ turned out to be, think about how advanced dogs are in the area of emotional intelligence. Not only do they sense the minute and subtle indicators of our moods, they respond appropriately and in a very genuine way. If you're angry, your dog may cower under the table. When you're sad, he might come running over, showering you with physical affection. And if you're feeling great, he's probably more than happy to wag his tail and jump in the fun.

This is not to say dogs never misread signals or act in "uncivilized" ways. They've been with us for thousands of years (until recently, scientists estimated 15,000 years, but new DNA evidence suggests it may be closer to 100,000,) but the call of the wild is still a very strong call. Who knows what complicated amalgam of instinct, breeding, and training (not to mention the tension between these forces) leads to behaviours that leave us scratching our head? Sometimes, however, the seeming illogic of their ways may be very reasonable indeed. If a baby is crying and a dog barks incessantly, we get irritated with the dog and feel he is making the situation worse. Can't it be that the dog, aware of the baby's helplessness, is just trying in the best way he knows how to get it the attention it needs?

Dogs may bark at friends thinking they are intruders, at rowdy neighbourhood boys just having a good time, at insects, postmen, even at phantoms. But they also bark when a pan is burning on the stove or when a potentially threatening figure sneaks up behind you on a late-night walk. Like Lassie, they have a lot to say, and limited means of saying it. The limits, though, may really be ours. After all, a wolf in the wild knows the scent of aggression, of helplessness and fear. They understand the angle of the tail and the tone of a whimper. They can read the level of threat in eye contact, and know to keep their distance by the length and pitch of a growl.

Dogs have done a great deal to learn to live on our terms. We feed them and give them shelter, yes, but we still might wonder what makes them so wholly devoted to us in our world … given how little we've done to try to live in theirs. But maybe we'd do better just to thank them. And to remember that no matter what their functional IQs, they are far and away our superiors when it comes to advanced moral reasoning and philosophy. Towards that end I'll leave you with a canine credo: while many humans would agree that these principles are rational and true, very few among us act on them consistently, if at all. Certainly none of us with the unwavering faith and attention of just about any old rough and tumble playground mutt!

Canine Credo

1 Relationships come first.

2 Never put self-interest above love and duty.

3 Do not get angry at someone for an accident, even if you get hurt.

4 Games are for fun: don't gloat when you win and don't feel sorry for yourself if you lose. In both cases, start a new game.

5 Going outside is a great adventure, every day. Even if you just came in from going outside.

6 One person can be the most important to you, but your capacity for love is unlimited.

7 Don't be vain.

8 Don't be afraid to show affection.

9 Show true remorse when it's called for.

10 Don't complain.

11 Be friendly, but don't assume you can trust everybody.

12 Accept change.

13 Forgive loved ones readily.

14 Enjoy the simple things in life like an open window to gaze out of, a warm bed to sleep in, a visit from a friend, or a squeaky new toy.

Selected Bibliography

Bobby, Anne. *Love Me or Leash Me: 50 Simple Ways to Keep Me a Happy, Healthy and Well Behaved Companion.* Black Dog & Leventhal Publishers, 2001

Coren, Stanley. *The Intelligence of Dogs: A Guide to the Thoughts, Emotions, and Inner Lives of Our Canine Companions.* Free Press, 2005

Coren, Stanley. *How Dogs Think.* Pocket Books, 2005

Millan, Cesar. *Cesar's Way: The Natural, Everyday Guide to Understanding and Correcting Common Dog Problems.* Harmony, 2006

Miller, Melissa. *The Dog I.Q. Test.* Penguin, 1994

Sternberg, Robert J. *Beyond IQ: A Triarchic Theory of Human Intelligence.* Cambridge University Press, 1984

Wright, Sue Owens. *What's Your Dog's IQ?: How to Determine If Your Dog Is an Einstein—and What to Do If He's a Scooby Doo.* Adams Media Corporation, 2006